SKILLS

WRITTEN AND COMPILED BY
HUW TURBERVILL

MADCAP

The publisher would like to thank the following for their kind permission to reproduce their photographs:

b=below; c= centre; l=left; r=right; t=top;

John Peters (official photographer)

Front Cover
John Peters (official photographer)

FOOTBALL SKILLS

Greater demands than ever are being placed on the modern-day footballer. Fitness is arguably as important as talent. You need stamina and pace to survive ninety gruelling minutes in the Premiership – one of the most frantic and exciting leagues in the world. Players must train hard and eat a balanced diet.

Brilliant ball skills are essential. You must be able to trap the ball and control it with both feet. Good distribution is vital. Long gone are the days when defenders were merely required to clear the ball from danger – now they are expected to carry the ball out of defence and start attacks.

Midfielders must be creative – they must be able to operate both in their own penalty area and in attack – while strikers must be good in the air and brave when sliding in on goal.

Ryan Giggs

You have to possess enormous skill and be adaptable if you want to play for a club like Manchester United. Do you fancy being the next Ryan Giggs? With dedication and hard work – coupled with talent – you might just get there.

GOALKEEPING SKILLS

A goalkeeper's task is to form a formidable barrier between an opponent and the goal he is guarding. His ability to read the game, anticipating the next move and positioning himself accordingly, gives him a vital advantage over the opponent.

Narrowing the angle

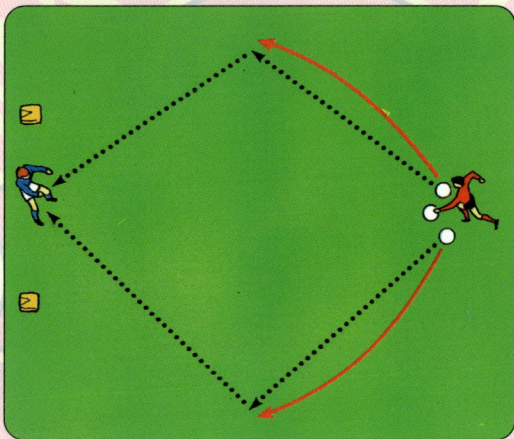

Ask a friend to play striker, while you practise in goal.

■ Move towards the ball.

■ Protect the near-post first.

■ Try to remain on your feet for as long as possible, spreading yourself and not committing until your opponent makes his first move. This shot-stopping technique is the hallmark of a truly outstanding goalkeeper, since most allow themselves to be fooled by the attacker.

GOALKEEPING SKILLS

Once the ball is in the goalkeeper's hands, United can be on the attack. How many times have we seen Peter Schmeichel launch a mighty long-distance throw into the opponents' half to create a goal-scoring opportunity for the Reds? It could be a throw to send Ryan Giggs on his way down the left flank, or it might be even more direct, allowing Andy Cole a run at goal. Either way, when the goalie has the ball in his hands, every team-mate is on alert – and opponents are on their guard.

Starting an attack out of defence
(overarm throw)

■ To throw out of defence, take the ball in your hand, keeping a straight arm, and point the other arm and leading leg towards your target. Cradle the ball against your inner wrist to balance it.

■ Keeping the arm that is supporting the ball straight and stiff, and hips swivelled towards the target, swing the throwing arm over in an arc.

■ All your weight will go on the leading leg and the non-throwing arm will now point towards the ground. The faster you throw and the larger the arc, the further the ball will travel.

GOALKEEPING SKILLS

Premiership stars can strike the ball with real venom, so the goalkeeper needs to make sure that he gets everything behind the ball.

Blocking a shot along the ground

■ Keep your eyes on the shot – NEVER take your eyes off the ball. If you become distracted and the ball takes a deflection, your opponents are sure to score.

■ Position yourself on one knee, with the other knee out supporting your weight. This provides an extra defence.

■ When the ball reaches you, scoop it up with both hands towards your chest. Make sure that you have the ball under control with both hands, otherwise lurking strikers may take advantage.

GOALKEEPING SKILLS

You need great agility to be a Premiership goalkeeper. The ability to leap swiftly into the air and deflect a high shot is vital.

Stopping a high shot

- Your hands should be slightly apart, with fingers spread out to form a 'W' shape.

- Jump off one leg to give yourself more height to clear the ball.

- Bend your forearms to help absorb the impact of the ball. Your fingers should be firm but relaxed.

- Once the ball touches your hands, bring them back together and use your chest to cushion the ball. Clutch the ball tightly, as nearby opponents will take advantage of any mistake.

General tips

- Use your height to control your penalty area, particularly at corners and crosses into the box.

- Although you need to be skilful with your hands, you have to be a capable last line of defence, often using your head or feet to clear the ball.

- Always try to catch the ball with two hands, but if you must punch, punch hard with both fists!

DEFENDING SKILLS

Gary Neville

Gary's concentration, his speed of thought and his immaculate timing have enabled him to establish himself with both club and country. His all-round ability as a defender has often shone through when he has been switched to a central role. He cannot afford to be caught off guard, and as a full-back he must keep a close eye on the opposition winger to ensure that he wins this personal battle.

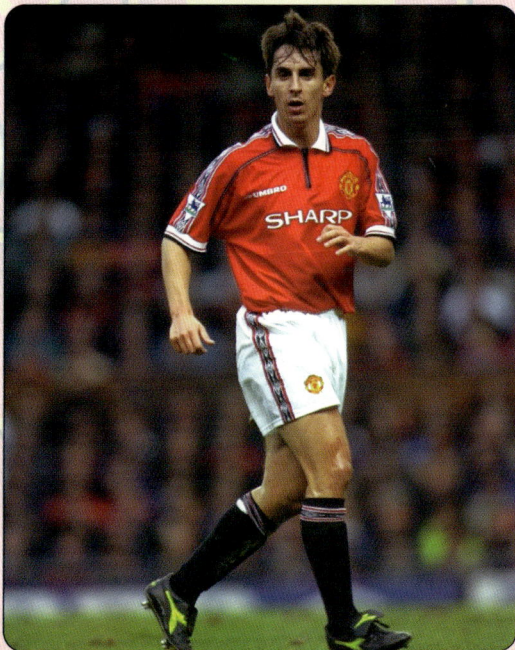

Gary Neville

DEFENDING SKILLS

Tackling

- Timing is essential when Gary commits himself to a tackle. He cannot afford to be reckless and must time his challenge to perfection. Failure to do so could result in a caution, a free-kick in a dangerous position, or even worse – a penalty!

- Gary will decide when he feels that his opponent has played the ball too far in front of him. Don't over-commit yourself, otherwise the attacker can take the ball past you and leave you lying on the grass!

- When you're ready to commit, move quickly and attack the middle and the front of the ball positively. Lift out your arms to balance yourself.

- Gary slides down low and keeps his leg wrapped around the ball. He uses his elbow to help him back on his feet, ready to pass the ball.

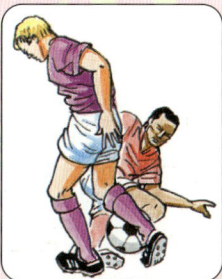

DEFENDING SKILLS

Jaap Stam

Jaap is a fine example of a modern-day central defender, physically strong, mentally alert and without any sign of panic with the ball at his feet. His ability on the ground is what persuaded United to pay a world-record fee for a defender, when they bought him for £10.6 million from the Dutch side PSV Eindhoven in the summer of 1998.

Jaap's strength in the tackle, along with his many other defence skills, such as his skilful headers, helped him to earn the title of Dutch Player of the Year before joining United – a sure sign of his all-round capabilities.

Jaap Stam

DEFENDING SKILLS

Taking the ball into the opponents' half

Like most of the best Continental defenders, Jaap is extremely strong at taking the ball out of defence and launching a United attack. Practise his skills for yourself.

- Speed is a key factor. As you push the ball forward, make sure that it is always within reach.

- Between touches, look to see where your team-mates (and opponents) are positioned. Use the outside of your foot to move the ball forward.

- After making the pass, make sure that you have cover in defence before advancing further forward in attack.

- If your run has not been covered by your team-mates, return rapidly to defence.

Passing to a team-mate

You can practise passing like Jaap by playing with two friends. One should be your team-mate and the other an opponent.

- Run with the ball until you are only a few feet away from your opponent, then look up to spot your team-mate.

- Pass the ball wide of your opponent, but just in front of your team-mate so that he can run on to the pass.

- After your pass, you can advance further up the pitch if your run has been covered defensively by your team-mate. Make yourself available for a return pass.

DEFENDING SKILLS

Ronny Johnsen

Ronny is a hard-working player who has an appetite for battle, and relishes the opportunity to tackle and win the ball in key areas. Also skilful as a central defender, he is blessed with an excellent temperament, often appearing calm in the most intense situations, and uses his ability in the air to good advantage.

At over 6 ft tall, when Johnsen operates in midfield he is useful at winning headers in front of his own defence, while posing a threat at the other end as United look to set pieces to create scoring chances.

Ronny has a useful turn of pace and a great sense of position, which can be a wonderful asset in both defensive and attacking situations.

Ronny Johnsen

DEFENDING SKILLS

Heading the ball out of defence

Ronny is powerful in the air. Practise your heading skills with a friend or against a wall.

- Make sure that you are in line with the flight of the ball.

- Keep your eye on the ball. Bend your knees slightly and hold your arms out for balance. If you need to, jump off one leg to gain extra height.

- Take back your head and the top half of your body, then push your body forward with the middle of your forehead meeting the ball. Keep your neck muscles stiff and your head firm. Head through the top half of the ball to keep it down.

- As an alternative to heading the ball powerfully out of defence, Ronny may also bring the ball under control by tilting his back slightly and letting it run down to his feet. Then a team-mate can move the ball away from defence.

FULLBACK SKILLS

Denis Irwin

It seems extraordinary now, bearing in mind his success for both club and country, that Denis was once among those players given a free transfer by a top club – in his case, Leeds. Their loss has turned out to be United's gain. Denis has long been recognised as one of the finest fullbacks in the country, and his value cannot be underestimated.

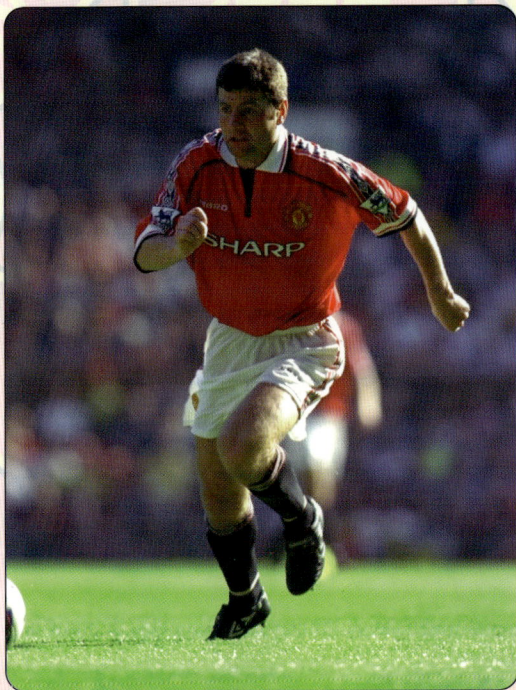

Denis Irwin

FULLBACK SKILLS

Quick, determined and excellent at supporting the attack with his forward runs and pinpoint centre shots, he is the complete fullback and goes about his task in an almost casual style. While Irwin relies on his ability to read the game to intercept danger, he is always ready to turn physical to challenge for possession.

Denis Irwin is United's expert penalty taker. He boasts an enviable record, and his accuracy from dead-ball situations has been further proved by a string of 'wonder goals' from free kicks taken well outside the area.

Taking a penalty

Like Denis, you must be decisive when taking penalties. Penalties often decide the outcome of a game.

■ Some players just hit the ball as hard as they can and hope for the best, but the more skilful penalty takers know which area of the goal they're aiming for.

■ It's a battle of wits against the goalkeeper. Most keepers choose which way, either left or right, they are going to dive. They know the odds are stacked against them – nobody expects a keeper to save a penalty – which means the pressure is on you, the penalty taker.

■ The modern trend is to hit the ball powerfully into the middle of the net – a goalkeeper will rarely stay upright in the middle of the goal.

MIDFIELD SKILLS

David Beckham

David is a gifted footballer with a vast range of skills, whether he's in a central role or on the right of midfield. He's deadly when taking a free kick outside the box – as he has consistently shown in action for United, and perhaps most memorably when he scored for England against Columbia in the World Cup finals of 1998.

Breathtaking free kicks have become something of a trademark for David, but no United fan will forget the long-distance goal he scored at Wimbledon on the opening day of the 1997-98 season. It was an inspired moment as he looked up, spotted the goalkeeper had strayed off his line, and, from a distance of 57 yards, executed the perfect chip into the unguarded net.

David Beckham

MIDFIELD SKILLS

Beckham is an accomplished passer of the ball, over both short and long distances. While he has some special strikes of his own, he is acknowledged as United's leading provider of goals, courtesy of his perfect crosses and defence-splitting passes.

Taking a free kick

- As you run up to the ball, lean your weight on to your supporting leg. Keeping your balance, outstretch your arms slightly backwards.

- Lift your kicking leg into a high backswing, then turn your body towards the ball. Kick the lower arc of the ball with the inside of your right foot, actually curling your foot into the ball to create a swerve.

- Beckham is able to both bend and strike the ball over the defensive wall, doing so with speed, and ensuring that it comes down quickly enough to hit the target.

MIDFIELD SKILLS

Nicky Butt

Nicky's ability to slot straight into the United first team was one of Alex Ferguson's reasons for allowing Paul Ince to depart for Italian club Inter Milan in the summer of 1995. This proved Ferguson's confidence in the youngster's all-round midfield skills, both as a combative ball winner and as a more creative player with an eye for a killer pass.

Butt doesn't stop to admire his handiwork – he races forward towards the opposition's penalty box, going on to score or create a chance for a team-mate. He occupies an anchoring role, always aware of his defensive responsibilities.

Nicky Butt

MIDFIELD SKILLS

Turning defence into an attack

■ Concentrate on making a crisp tackle. Don't over-commit: pick your moment and make your movement swift.

■ Don't just pass the ball to the first team-mate you see. Look for ways to progress forward or open up the opponents' defence.

■ Once he's made the pass, Nicky never stands there and admires it. Like him, look to join the attack or help cover in defence.

WINGER SKILLS

Ryan Giggs

There are few finer sights in football than seeing Ryan Giggs in full flight, torturing fullbacks with his close control, lightning pace and ability to shoot on the run.

Ryan Giggs

Giggs is special because he is capable of doing with ease what only a very few players in the world can do – taking on and dribbling past opponents, then creating an end product in the shape of a pinpointed cross or an attempt at goal.

One of Ryan's specialities is to race down the left, trick his direct opponent and then turn inside on his right foot and send a curling shot from the edge of the box, beyond the outstretched arms of the opposition goalkeeper and into the far corner of the net.

WINGER SKILLS

Dribbling

Ryan uses a number of tricks to beat an opponent.

- When he is being closed down, Ryan will often sway out of the way and take the ball in a different direction. Try this move for yourself.

- Use your head and body to make it look as if you mean to play the ball.

- If your opponent moves to cover this 'feint', use the inside of your standing foot to play the ball in the opposite direction.

Crossing

- Ryan will beat an opponent and then look up to see if a team-mate is in the clear.

- He whips the ball to his team-mate with just the right amount of curve to tempt a goalkeeper to leave his line and try to reach it. The goalkeeper will almost always be left floundering, giving United's attackers a chance to gain the upper hand.

ALL-ROUND SKILLS

Roy Keane

This is what Alex Ferguson has to say about the United captain: "Roy has a superb knowledge of the game, awareness, vision, passing ability, an incredible engine and is a great competitor."

Often described as the most complete player in the country, Roy is a three-in-one player – defender, midfielder and attacker in an explosive package.

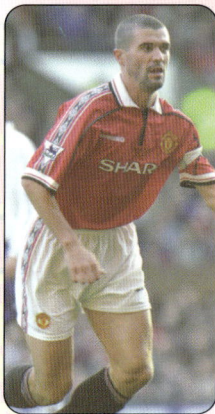

Roy Keane

Chest trap

Roy is a ball-winner, and he will often use his chest to trap a loose ball in midfield. The chest trap is a very useful technique when the ball is approaching at a level height or rising.

■ Move yourself into the flight-path of the ball, positioning your chest over the ball.

■ Extend your chest out towards the ball. When you make contact, snap

ALL-ROUND SKILLS

your shoulders forward
to make an absorbent
surface for the ball.
At the same time, tilt
the trunk of your body
forward to direct the
ball down.

Inside foot flick

Roy often uses an inside
foot flick to lay the ball off.

■ Face the ball with your back to the target.

■ When the ball is level with your
controlling foot, flick it back behind the
foot that you are standing on.

■ Your standing foot will be slightly in front
of your playing foot, so the ball will
move diagonally.

STRIKER SKILLS

Paul Scholes

Paul is equipped with one of the most alert football brains of any player in United's history. He represents an almost unique combination of hard work and subtle skills. His preferred position is behind the main strikers and he is a real handful for opponents, with managers unsure of how to cope with his presence.

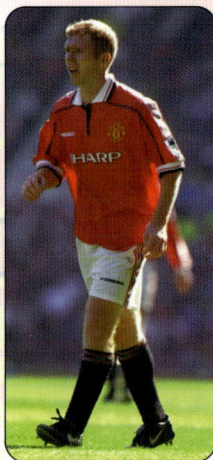

Paul Scholes

Scholes is an ideal link man, brilliant at exploiting space. Former England coach Glenn Hoddle paid him a huge compliment when he said: "There isn't a player of his mould anywhere in the world."

No matter how tight the situation, Paul usually has the answer. He can operate as a traditional midfielder, careful when tackling and gifted when it comes to distributing the ball. When used further forward, he carries a scoring threat and likes nothing more than to let fly with shots from outside the area.

Paul is always looking for ways to deceive opponents. Here are two ways you can unlock defences using the element of surprise.

STRIKER SKILLS

Back-heel pass

- Use the back of your foot to nudge the ball behind and to a team-mate.

- Because you don't have a good view of where you're passing the ball, it's best to use this trick only occasionally.

- When it comes off, it can totally confuse a defence and lead to a goal-scoring opportunity.

Dummy

Paul uses a dummy pass to fool defenders.

- Move towards the ball, as if you are about to play it.

- Move out of the way at the last possible moment. The defender will have shadowed your movements and will have very little chance to recover.

STRIKER SKILLS

Andy Cole

Since joining United, Andy has developed his overall game to become a well-rounded player. He has become a key ingredient in United's build-up play, as well as being something of an assassin in front of goal.

Cole packs a ferocious shot and has the agility to leap above opposition defenders and reach corners, free kicks and crosses aimed towards him from either side.

Andy Cole

Sliding ground shot

Andy is an expert at meeting crosses.

STRIKER SKILLS

- He runs in towards goal. When he is about to make contact with the ball, he starts to slide in on the leg that is nearest to the defender. Carefully try this for yourself.

- Slide in as far as you can reach, using your arm to support you.

- With a scooping action, steer the ball past the keeper and into the goal.

Shaking off defenders

Andy is obviously very closely marked, and has the ability to shake off defenders. You can practise this with two friends, one pretending to be a team-mate and the other an opponent.

- Run towards your team-mate who has the ball, encouraging the defender to follow you.

- Just before your team-mate passes to you, quickly make a change of direction, perhaps swerving backwards and a little to the side. Try to confuse the defender.

- Your team-mate will realise what you have done and will feed the ball past the beaten defender.

STRIKER SKILLS

Dwight Yorke

Dwight Yorke's pace and body strength set him apart from other strikers.

Playing for much of the game with his back to the goal, Yorke can keep the ball up and retain possession. His quick feet and turn of pace generally prove too strong for the opposition, and he has often scored extravagant goals, with overhead kicks, explosive shots or cheeky chips over a bewildered goalkeeper.

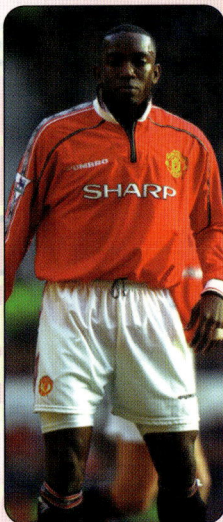

Dwight Yorke

Working in tandem with Andy Cole, Dwight has the ability to draw defenders away from his partner, allowing him a shot on goal.

Drawing defenders wide

■ Before Dwight's team-mate passes, he makes a run to give the player an option to pass.

STRIKER SKILLS

- By running wide, his team-mate can either pass to Dwight, setting him up for a cross or a shot on goal, or he can play through the defence, which is now a defender short.

Scissors overhead kick

Dwight has an eye for a spectacular goal, and he is skilled at the scissors overhead kick. Practise it for yourself, but TAKE CARE – this is a dangerous move.

- Try a scissors overhead kick when you have your back to the goal and a low, hard cross is coming over.

- When you are beneath the ball, bend your knees ready to jump. Allow your body to fall back gently, at the same time forcefully swinging up the foot that you are NOT going to kick the ball with.

- When it is as high as the ball, bring it down and swing your kicking leg up. Kick the ball over your shoulder

(which should be lower than the ball). Be very careful how you fall!

STRIKER SKILLS

Ole Gunnar Solskjaer

Ole may look slender, but he is deceptively strong in possession. He is very difficult to mark, shielding the ball so well that opposition defenders, however much taller and heavier they are, cannot get to it without resorting to a foul.

Ole's speciality is his eye for goal – he marked his first season at Old Trafford by becoming the leading goal scorer, netting 19 times from just 35 senior starts.

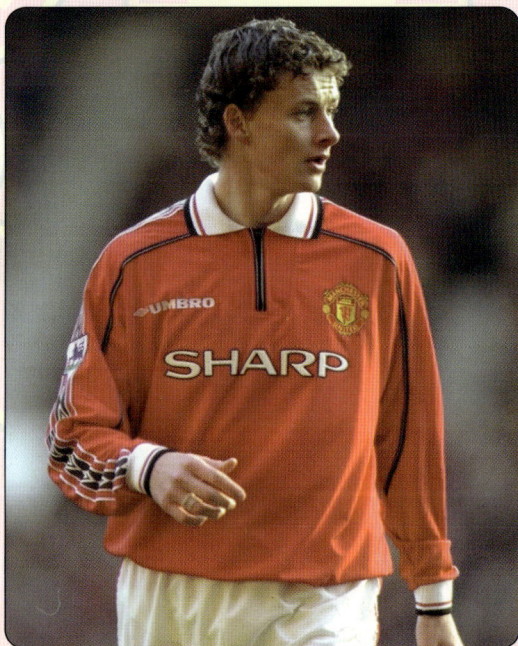

Ole Gunnar Solskjaer

STRIKER SKILLS

Diving header

Ole is known for his bravery and he grabs crucial goals from diving headers.

- Ole will meet a low-flying ball with a diving header. Try it for yourself.

- Throw yourself forward horizontally to the ground, with your arms stretched out in front.

- Keep your eyes focused on the ball. Use the top part of your forehead to project the ball and prevent it from going over the crossbar.

- Support yourself with your arms when you land. Ensure you have a soft fall.

Volleying

Ole is also skilful at volleying the ball. You need precision to strike the ball while it is in the air like Ole does.

- Get your knee and head over the ball and swing back your leg.

- Because you use the power already on the ball from the cross, you rarely need to follow through.

Manager Skills

Alex Ferguson

Alex Ferguson is one of United's finest managers. As manager of Aberdeen, he shattered Celtic's and Rangers' dominance of Scottish football. He also led Aberdeen to the European Cup Winners' Cup.

Success soon followed at Old Trafford when he took over in 1986. Alex has firmly moved the Red Devils out of the long shadow cast by the brilliance of arch rivals Liverpool during the 1980s.

To be a Premiership manager, you need:

- the ability to motivate your team.

- to know when to rest your players, when to change a team around, and when to bring on a substitute.

- to know when to dip into the transfer market. Ferguson has a fantastic eye for a player, with many successful purchases to date.

- to nurture young talent: Ryan Giggs, David Beckham, the Neville brothers, Paul Scholes, Nicky Butt, Wes Brown and John Curtis have all flourished under Ferguson's leadership.

- to have a style of management which commands respect from the players.